Girlology

SOCIAL MEDIA SAVVY

Facts and figures about selfies, smartphones and standing out

Elizabeth Raum

raintree

a Capstone company — publishers for children

Raintree is an imprint of Capstone Global Library Limited, a company incorporated in England and Wales having its registered office at 264 Banbury Road, Oxford, OX2 7DY - Registered company number: 6695582

www.raintree.co.uk myorders@raintree.co.uk

Edited by Mandy Robbins
Designed by Kayla Rossow
Original illustrations © Capstone Global Library Limited 2018
Picture research by Jo Miller
Production by Kathy McColley
Originated by Capstone Global Library Ltd Printed and bound in India

ISBN 978 1 4747 4809 4 (hardcover)
22 21 20 19 18
10 9 8 7 6 5 4 3 2 1

ISBN 978 1 4747 4817 9 (paperback)
23 22 21 20 19
10 9 8 7 6 5 4 3 2 1

British Library Cataloguing in Publication Data
A full catalogue record for this book is available from the British Library.

Acknowledgements
Getty Images: John Lamparski/Contributor, 20, The Washington Post/Contributor, 21; Shutterstock: Antonio Guillem, 18, Antun Hirsman, 24-25, cunaplus, 30b, DisobeyArt, 4l, Fine Art, 22r, g-stockstudio, 4r, George Rudy, 13, Iakov Filimonov, 23, iofoto, 11, Leszek Czerwonka, 16-17, MPFphotography, 8, Nitikorn Poonsiri, 30t, Odua Images, 26, oneinchpunch, 27, rangizzz, 9t, Rawpixel.com, 12, 19, Rohappy, 9bl, SpeedKingz, 28, 29, Stuart Jenner, 22b, Syrytsyna Tetiana, 7, 22m, vovan, 9br

Design Elements
Capstone Studio: Karon Dubke; Shutterstock: AD Hunter, Angie Makes, Antun Hirsman, blackzheep, Bloomicon, Mariam27, MPFphotography, optimarc, In-Finity

Printed and bound in India.

CONTENTS

Chapter 1

SOCIAL MEDIA IN OUR LIVES

Social media is your electronic communication lifeline. The majority of people on social media connect with mobile devices. What's your favourite way to stay connected?

HOW DO MOST PEOPLE STAY CONNECTED?

80%: smartphones, tablets, smart watches and other mobile devices

20%: desktop, laptop and notebook computers and games consoles

80% 20%

WHO'S ON THE INTERNET?

A better question might be "Who's not?" The internet is a worldwide phenomenon, but there are some places where internet use is more widespread than others.

Internet use by region of the world

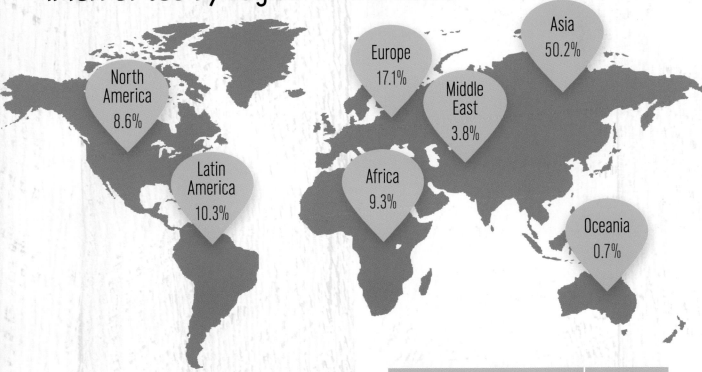

North America 8.6%

Europe 17.1%

Asia 50.2%

Middle East 3.8%

Latin America 10.3%

Africa 9.3%

Oceania 0.7%

Compare the percentage of internet use shown above with the percentage of the world's population that each of these regions make up.

Region	Percentage of the world's population	Percentage of internet use
Asia	55.2%	50.2%
Europe	10.9%	17.1%
Latin America	8.6%	10.3%
Africa	16.6%	9.3%
North America	4.8%	8.6%
Middle East	3.3%	3.8%
Oceana	0.5%	0.7%

WHO USES SOCIAL MEDIA?

Almost everyone! The majority of people who use the internet have at least one social media profile.

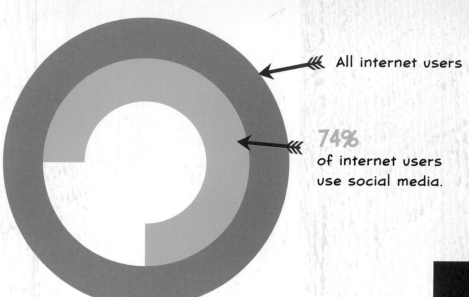

All internet users

74%
of internet users use social media.

Boys and girls tend to spend their time on the internet in different ways, particularly when it comes to gaming and social media.

■ = social media   ■ = video games

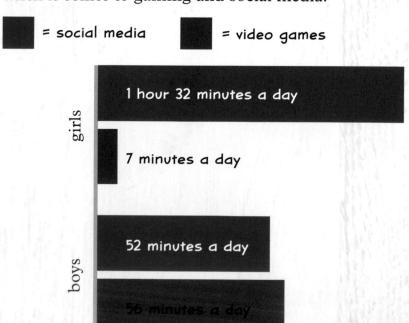

girls
1 hour 32 minutes a day

7 minutes a day

boys
52 minutes a day

56 minutes a day

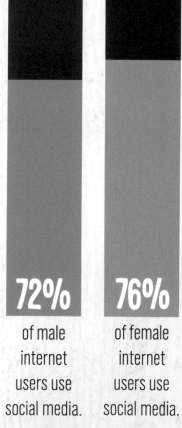

72%
of male internet users use social media.

76%
of female internet users use social media.

SOCIAL MEDIA BY AGE

Internet and social media usage varies with age. Understandably, people who didn't grow up using the internet don't use it as much as younger people.

Percentage of people on social media

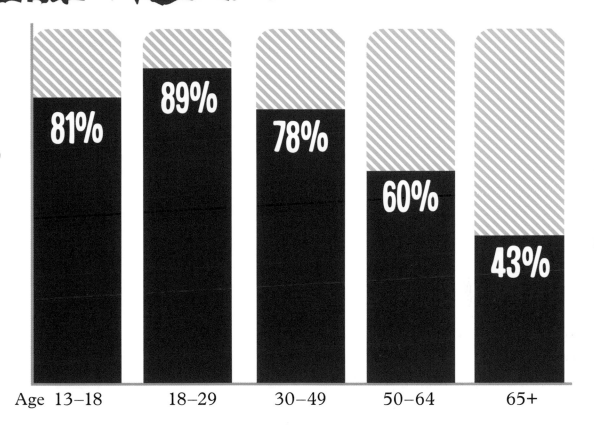

| 81% | 89% | 78% | 60% | 43% |
| Age 13–18 | 18–29 | 30–49 | 50–64 | 65+ |

How much time are children your age spending on social media or watching videos on sites such as YouTube?

Ages 8 to 12 average 6 hours a day.

Ages 13 to 18 average 9 hours a day.

TEXTING IS TOPS

Texting, whether it's through social media or directly from phone to phone, is a favourite method of communication among teenagers. In 2015, the New York Times found that teenagers send, on average, 60 texts a day. Girls send closer to 100 texts, and boys send about 50. How do your texting habits compare?

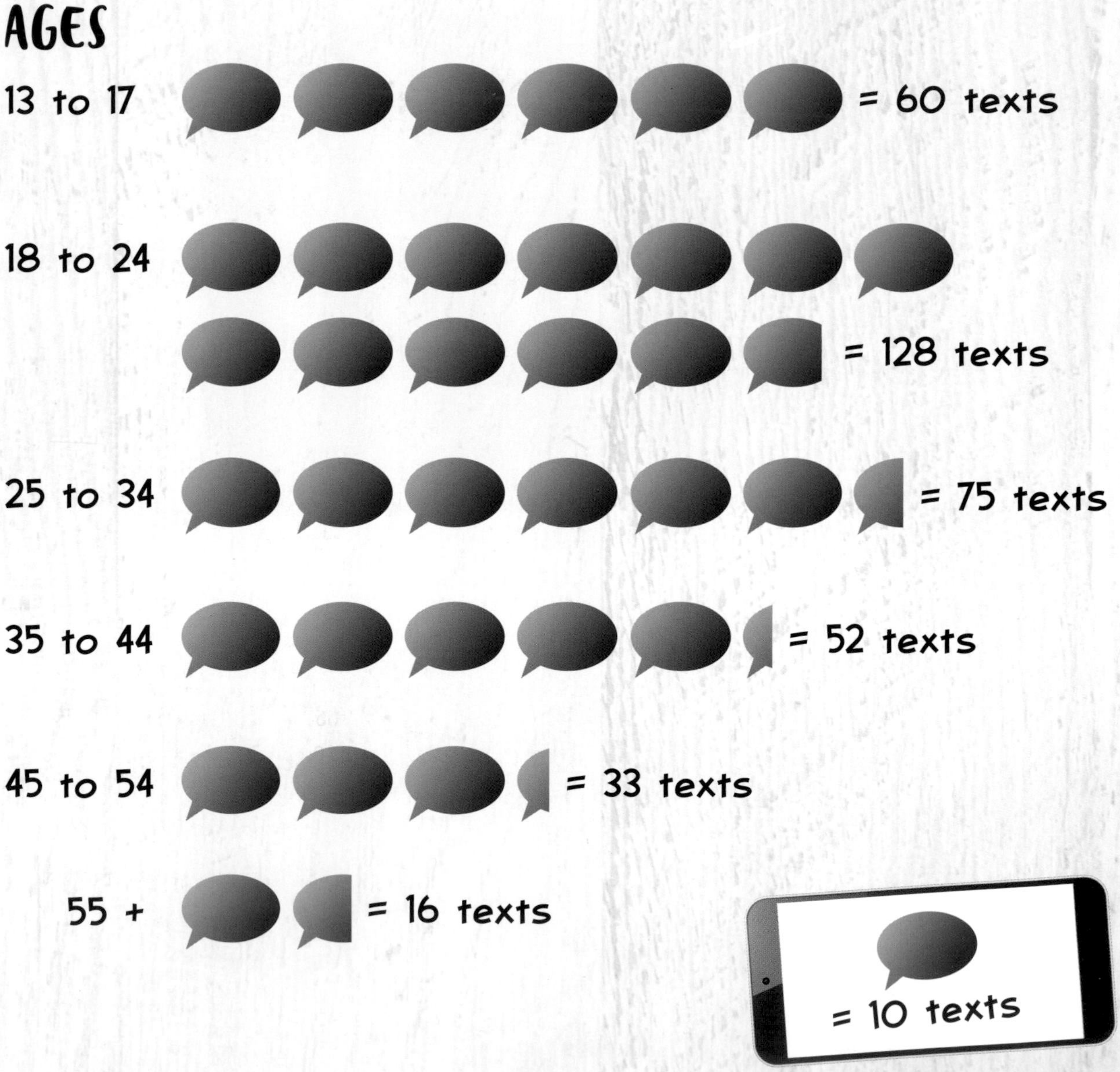

AGES

13 to 17 = 60 texts

18 to 24 = 128 texts

25 to 34 = 75 texts

35 to 44 = 52 texts

45 to 54 = 33 texts

55 + = 16 texts

= 10 texts

8

Texting is great! It's quicker than calling someone, and you can message multiple people at the same time. But then you knew that. But you might not know these fun factoids:

90 seconds: the average response time for a text.

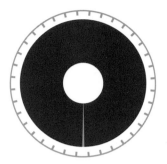  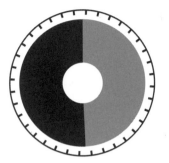

99% of texts are read.

95% of texts are read within 3 minutes of being sent.

51% of teenagers would rather communicate digitally than in person.

TEXTING VS PHONE CALLS

26 minutes: the average amount of time people spend texting every day

6 minutes: the average amount of time people spend talking on the phone every day

So with all this texting, is anyone actually talking to each other on their phones?

 Yes, but it's getting less and less.

88 the average number of text messages people aged between 18-29 send every day

17 the average number of phone calls people aged between 18-29 make every day

Chapter 2

SOCIAL MEDIA PLATFORMS

Social media platforms have come a long way in the last 20 years. The first, called Six Degrees, was created in 1997. Today there are many social media sites, but a few are a real hit with teenagers. Instagram and Snapchat are among the most popular.

WHAT SOCIAL MEDIA PLATFORMS DO TEENS USE?

* Data is based on teenagers aged 13 to 17.

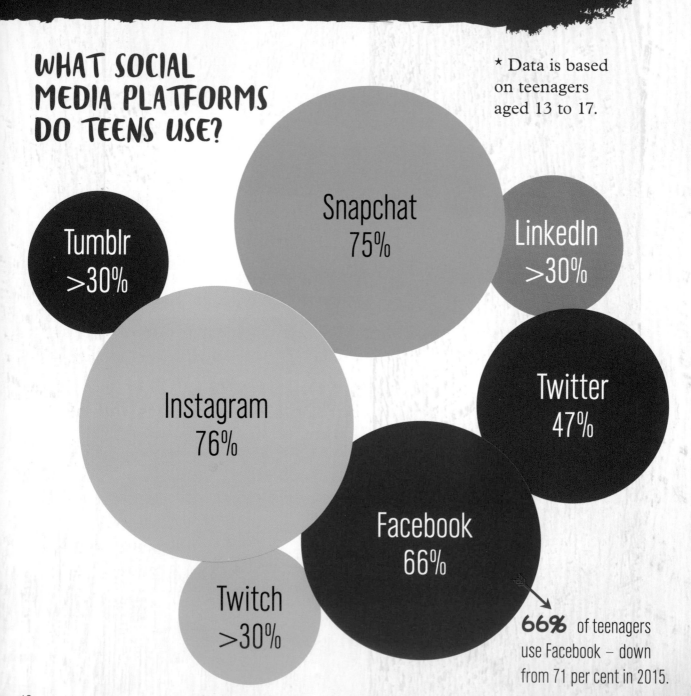

Tumblr
>30%

Snapchat
75%

LinkedIn
>30%

Instagram
76%

Twitter
47%

Facebook
66%

Twitch
>30%

66% of teenagers use Facebook – down from 71 per cent in 2015.

WHAT ARE THE RESTRICTIONS?

Social media sites have minimum age requirements. Do you know what they are?

Twitter Reddit	YouTube	LinkedIn	WhatsApp
Facebook Snapchat	WeChat		
Instagram Steam	Foursquare		
Pinterest Twitch	Flickr		
Google+ Path	Kik		
age: **13**	**13** (w/parents' permission)	**14**	**16**

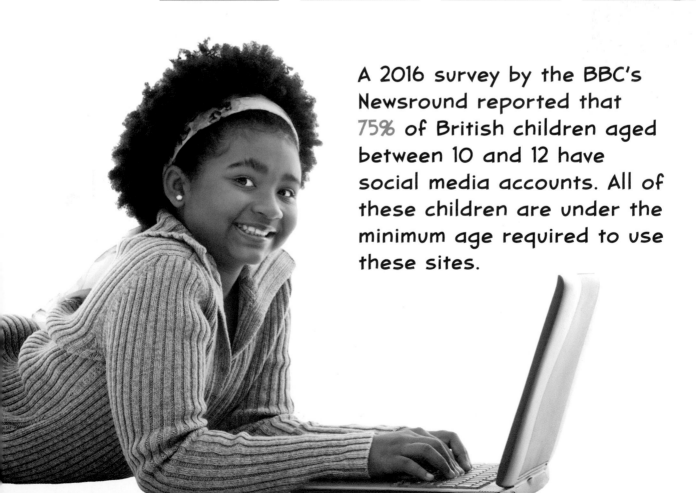

A 2016 survey by the BBC's Newsround reported that 75% of British children aged between 10 and 12 have social media accounts. All of these children are under the minimum age required to use these sites.

MOST POPULAR SOCIAL MEDIA PLATFORMS FOR TEENS BY GENDER

67.9% 66.7% 47.7% 34.9% 40.3%

Teenage girls

Instagram
Snapchat
Facebook

Twitter
Google+

51.9%   46.6%   57.6%   35.9%   44%

Teenage boys

MILLIONS AND BILLIONS

Social media users flood cyberspace with text messages, videos and posts. The numbers surrounding various media platforms might surprise you. They stretch into the millions, billions and trillions!

Instagram

300 million
selfies posted

500 million
active monthly users

£1.15 billion
made from advertisers every year

4.2 billion
posts liked every day

40 billion
photographs uploaded since 2010

95 million
photos and videos shared every day

YouTube

3.25 billion
hours of video watched every month

1 billion
mobile video views every day

Snapchat

1 million snaps
created every day

100 million
daily users

300+ million
active monthly users

400+ million
Snapchat stories
created every day

10+ billion
Snapchat daily videos views

Twitter

- **23 million** fake accounts
- 310 million monthly users
- **500 million** tweets sent every day
- 500 million monthly visits without logging in
- **1.3 billion accounts**
  created since 2006

Facebook

16 million small businesses have Facebook pages

83 million fake profiles

300 million photos uploaded every day

1.15 billion mobile daily active users

1.32 billion users log on every day

2.01 billion active users worldwide

Chapter 3

SOCIAL MEDIA SAVVY

Test your social media IQ with these fast facts. Did you know that two of the three most visited websites are social media sites? They are Google, Facebook and YouTube. See if any of these other facts surprise you.

You can navigate YouTube in 76 different languages.

Every minute, 510,000 comments are posted on Facebook.

More than 20,000 photos are shared on Snapchat every second.

There are 300 hours of video uploaded to YouTube every minute.

Five new Facebook profiles are created every second.

Instagram users from Makati City and Pasig, Philippines, take the most "selfies" — 258 per 100,000 people.

"Charlie bit my finger" is the user-submitted YouTube video with the most views.

It would take 10 years to view all the photos put on Snapchat in 1 hour.

Every minute, 293,000 statuses are updated on Facebook.

Every minute, 136,000 photos are uploaded to Facebook.

In Nice, France, there are 30 selfie-takers per 100,000 people. The city is 100th on the list of cities with the most selfie-takers.

PINBOARDS, DISCUSSION BOARDS AND BLOGS

Pinboards are online sites like Pinterest and Polyvore. Users "pin" visual content to create displays. Discussion boards like Reddit or Digg provide a place for users to exchange opinions or mini-blogs.

FUN PINTEREST FACTS

175 million active monthly users.

The average pin is repinned **11 times.**

85% of users are female.

12% of Pinterest searches contain a spelling mistake.

There are more than **75 billion** pins on **1.5 billion boards.**

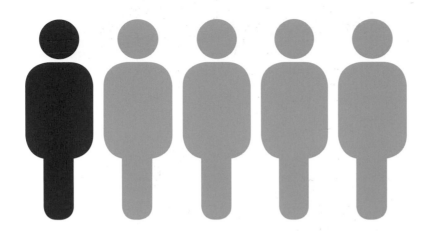

One in *five* teenagers use pinboards.

17%

of teenagers read or comment on discussion boards such as Reddit or Digg.

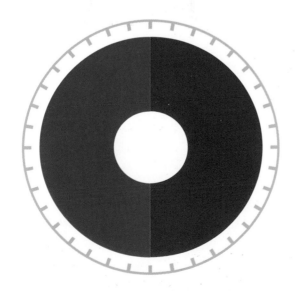

An equal number of boys and girls visit discussion boards.

MEMES

Have you heard the saying, "A picture is worth a thousand words"? Memes take that idea to the next level. These photos or videos are paired with text that can be funny, political or informative. You've probably seen lots of them. Anyone can make a meme, and they are passed from person to person. The best of the best go viral.

BEHIND THE MEMES

Memes can be hilarious! But have you ever wondered about the people or animals in them? They're more than just an image. So who are they?

Grumpy Cat
Real name: Tardar Sauce
Date of birth: 4 April 2012
Tardar Sauce took the internet by storm in 2012. Her grumpy expression paired with text such as, "I had fun once ... It was awful," inspired many more pet lovers to create funny memes of their own bad-tempered pets.

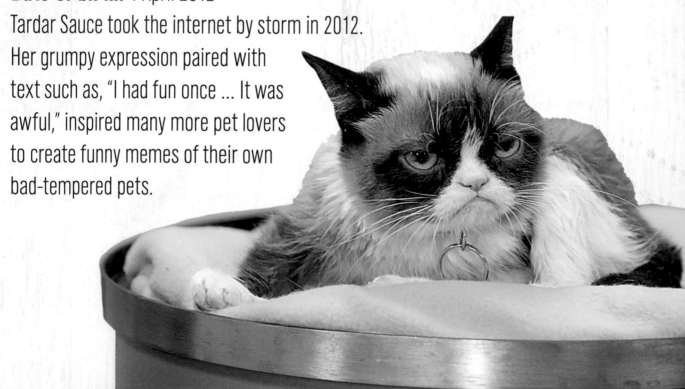

Bad Luck Brian

Real name: Kyle Craven

Date of birth: 10 August 1989

Kyle Craven's friends got hold of one of his school photos, and it set the internet on fire! Photo captions with "Bad Luck Brian" often muse about awful luck. For example, "Goes surfing for the first time … hurricane." The Bad Luck Brian meme became so popular that Kyle created a Bad Luck Brian YouTube channel. As of October 2017, it had more than 56,000 subscribers.

Success Kid

Real name: Sammy Griner

Date of birth: 23 September 2006

Have you seen the photo of the toddler in the white and green t-shirt pumping his fist? His face often accompanies words of unlikely accomplishments. One example is "Put five dollars in pocket...pull out ten." Sammy's family used the popularity of the meme to fundraise £75,000 to pay for his father's kidney transplant surgery in 2015.

VIDEOS ON SOCIAL MEDIA

Videos are a growing part of social media. Sites such as YouTube were made purely for the purposes of sharing videos, but video sharing is now an option on virtually every social media platform.

By 2019:
80% of internet traffic around the world will involve videos.

1 million minutes

of videos are shared online every **second.** That's **3.6 billion videos** every hour.

It would take
5 million years

to watch all the videos shared online in a month. To put that into perspective, that would be **50,000 centuries!**

YOUTUBE BASICS
Founded in 2004
Users watch 3.2 billion hours of YouTube videos every month.
1.5 billion logged-in monthly users.
180.1 million people in the US use YouTube.

TEENS ON YOUTUBE

91%
77%
64%
50%
49%

91% of internet users aged 13-17 use YouTube.

77% of teenagers subscribe to a YouTube channel.

64% of teenagers share YouTube videos on Facebook.

50% of teenagers look for YouTube videos that are funny.

49% of teenagers have uploaded a YouTube video.

THE ECONOMICS OF SOCIAL MEDIA

Social media is big business for advertisers. More and more advertising money is spent on social media every year.

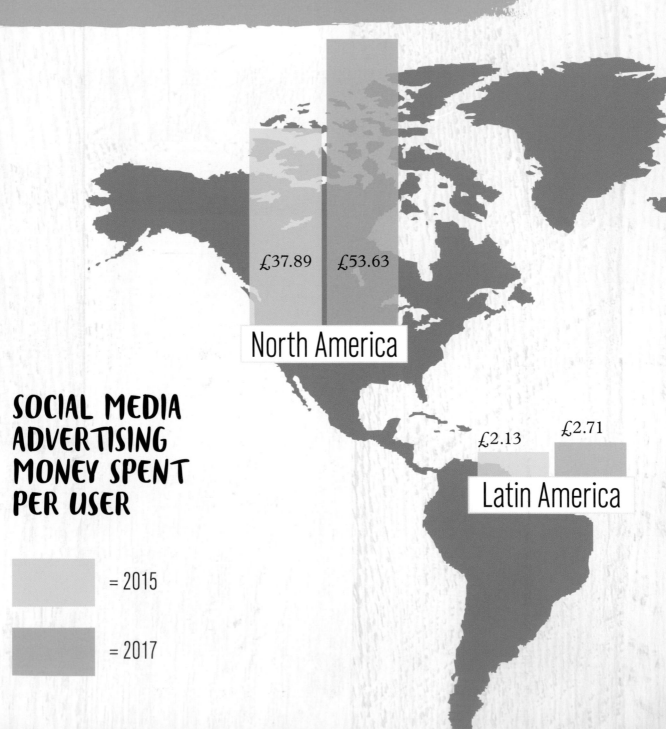

£37.89   £53.63

North America

£2.13   £2.71

Latin America

SOCIAL MEDIA ADVERTISING MONEY SPENT PER USER

	= 2015
	= 2017

The advertising money spent on social media has
made these businesses **BILLIONs** of pounds!

Social media site	Year founded	Estimated worth
Snapchat	2011	£11.46 billion
Twitter	2006	£8.88 billion
Facebook and Instagram (jointly owned)	2004	£367.90 billion

*numbers current as of 3 August 2017

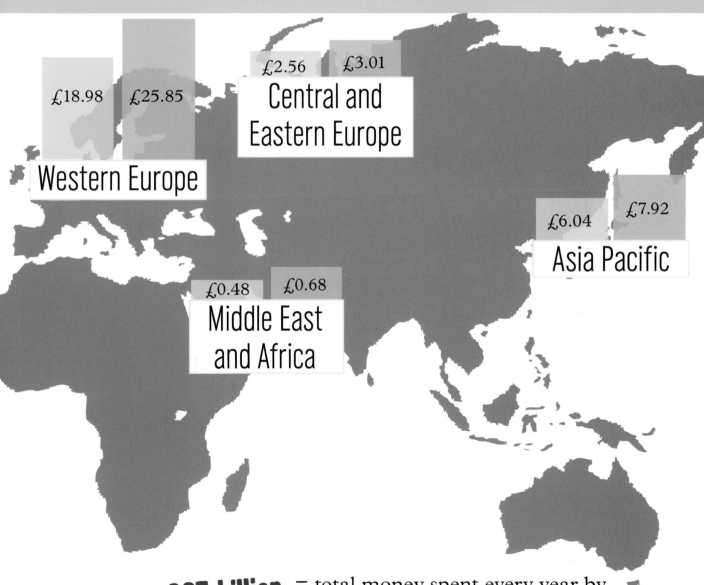

£18.98   £25.85

£2.56   £3.01

Central and
Eastern Europe

Western Europe

£6.04   £7.92

Asia Pacific

£0.48   £0.68

Middle East
and Africa

£27 billion = total money spent every year by
advertisers on social media.

Chapter 4

PROTECT YOUR ONLINE PRIVACY

Only **9%** of teenagers claim to be worried about privacy on social media.

However, **60%** keep their Facebook setting private.

SIX WAYS TO PROTECT YOUR PRIVACY ONLINE:

1. Use social media privacy settings.
2. Only communicate with people on social media who you know in real life.
3. Don't log in to other websites using your social media log-ins. Once you do, those websites can access your information.
4. Don't reveal personal information, such as your last name, phone number or home address.
5. Log out when you leave a social media website.
6. Remember that whatever you post online may be seen by strangers as well as people you know.

WHAT ARE YOU SHARING?

Everything you share online tells people something about yourself. See how your posts compare to those of other teenagers.

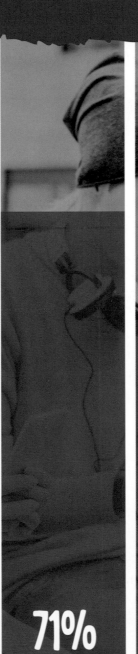

91%	71%	71%	53%	20%
photos of themselves	their school's name	the city or town where they live	email address	mobile phone number

DIGITAL DANGERS AND DISTRACTIONS

Cyberbullying is a real problem among teenagers. In a 2016 survey of 5,707 US students aged between 12 and 17, students reported that:

33.8%	had been a victim of cyberbullying at some time in their lives
22.5%	had seen unkind or hurtful comments online
20.1%	had read rumours online
12.7%	had seen posts about themselves containing unkind names or sexually explicit content
12.2%	had been threatened online
10.3%	had their identity used online by others without their consent
10.1%	had seen nasty comments online about their race or ethnicity
7.4%	had an unkind or hurtful video about them posted online
7.1%	had seen an unkind or hurtful web page made about them
10.3%	had missed school because of online bullying

60% of students felt that online bullying affected their ability to learn and feel safe!

COMBAT CYBERBULLIES!

If you or a friend are ever the target of a cyberbully, **ConnectSafely.org** offers some tips to help.

1. Don't respond. Sometimes the best thing to do is ignore the bully.

2. Don't retaliate. That just keeps the cycle of bullying going.

3. Save the evidence. Proof is power, especially if the bullying gets serious enough that you need to go to the authorities.

4. Talk to a trusted adult. They can be there to back you up and help you decide how to handle the situation.

5. Block the bully. If you can change your privacy settings to get a bully out of your life, do it!

6. Be civil. Even if you don't like someone, it's always best to be the bigger person. Don't sink to the level of a bully.

7. Don't BE the bully. Think before you post something on social media or text message someone. Would you be hurt if someone said the same thing about or to you?

8. Be a friend, not a bystander. Stand up to bullies! Don't forward on their messages or share cruel posts.

YUCK! THATS DISGUSTING!

Social media communities provide hours of fun. But did you know thriving communities of germs live on your smartphone? Check out these dirty facts.

Newsflash: Your mobile phone is 10 times more germ-ridden than most toilet seats.

BAD BATHROOM HABITS

You wouldn't believe what some people admit to doing with their phones in the bathroom.

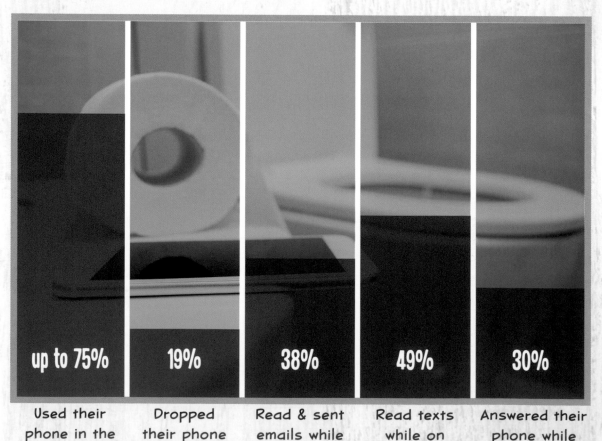

up to 75%	19%	38%	49%	30%
Used their phone in the bathroom	Dropped their phone in the toilet	Read & sent emails while on the toilet	Read texts while on the toilet	Answered their phone while on the toilet

GERMS PER SQUARE CENTIMETRE

You might be surprised to find out what the germiest places and items in your home are. Then again, you might not be. Where did you expect your mobile phone to appear in this list?

Common household items	Germs per square cm
computer mouse	8
computer keyboard	10
TV remote control	11
toilet flush	13
toilet seat	46
kitchen worktop	76
bathroom floor in front of the toilet	118
kitchen floor in front of the sink	129
kitchen tap handle	2,050
mobile phone	**3,875**
kitchen sponge	20,868

RECIPE FOR A CLEAN PHONE

You will need:
225 ml white vinegar
225 ml distilled water*

1. Mix the liquids in a small spray bottle.
2. Spray a soft cloth and wipe down the phone.
3. Use a cotton bud or a toothpick to clean the gunk out of the cracks between the glass cover and the phone's case.

Do this often. Your phone will be much cleaner!

* You must use distilled water. Tap water can leave a residue on the phone.

Author bio

Elizabeth Raum is a full-time writer who has lived in 12 different cities and towns in 7 different states in the US. She currently lives in North Dakota, USA. Her favourite ways to stay in touch with friends and family are face-to-face visits, email, talking on the phone, texting and social media. She is fascinated by statistics and hopes you are too.

Books in this series:

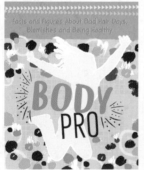

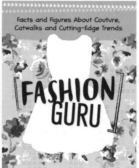

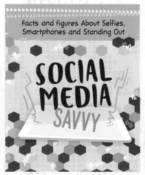

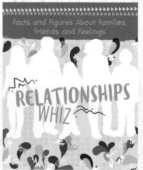